Valentine's Day

by **Trudi Strain Trueit**

Reading Consultant: Nanci R. Vargus, Ed.D.

Marshall Cavendish
Benchmark
New York

Picture Words

 balloons

 cards

chocolate

cookies

 cupcakes

 hearts

 lollipops

 sunglasses

Do you love to get
on Valentine's Day?

I love to get .

I love to get .

I love to get .

I love to get .

I love to get .

I love to get .

I love to get .

I love to give ♥♥♥, too.
Happy Valentine's Day!

Words to Know

love (LUV)
   to really like

Valentine's Day (VAL-ehn-tines DAY)
   a holiday on February 14 named
   for Saint Valentine and celebrated
   with flowers, candy hearts, and
   cards

Find Out More

Books

Boonyadhistarn, Thiranut. *Valentines: Cards and Crafts from the Heart*. Mankato, MN: Capstone Press, 2007.

McGee, Randel. *Paper Crafts for Valentine's Day*. Berkeley Heights, NJ : Enslow, 2008.

Otto, Carolyn. *Celebrate Valentine's Day*. New York, NY: Random House, 2007.

Websites

Making Friends.Com: Valentine's Day Crafts
www.makingfriends.com/valentine.htm

PBS KIDS: Valentine's Day Activities
http://pbskids.org/vday

About the Author

Valentine's Day is one of Trudi Strain Trueit's favorite holidays. (She loves candy hearts.) Trudi is the author of more than fifty fiction and nonfiction books for children, including *Thanksgiving* and *Halloween* in the Benchmark Rebus Holiday Fun series. Visit her website at **www.truditrueit.com**.

About the Reading Consultant

Nanci R. Vargus, Ed.D., wants all children to enjoy reading. She used to teach first grade. Now she works at the University of Indianapolis. Nanci helps young people become teachers. She loves exchanging valentines with her students and family.

Other Marshall Cavendish Offices:
Marshall Cavendish International (Asia) Private Limited, 1 New Industrial Road, Singapore 536196 • Marshall Cavendish International (Thailand) Co Ltd. 253 Asoke, 12th Flr, Sukhumvit 21 Road, Klongtoey Nua, Wattana, Bangkok 10110, Thailand • Marshall Cavendish (Malaysia) Sdn Bhd, Times Subang, Lot 46, Subang Hi-Tech Industrial Park, Batu Tiga, 40000 Shah Alam, Selangor Darul Ehsan, Malaysia

Marshall Cavendish is a trademark of Times Publishing Limited

All websites were available and accurate when this book was sent to press.

Library of Congress Cataloging-In-Publication Data
Trueit, Trudi Strain.
Valentine's day / Trudi Strain Trueit.
       p. cm. — (Benchmark rebus. Holiday fun)
Includes bibliographical references.
Summary: "A simple introduction to Valentine's Day using rebuses"—Provided by publisher.
ISBN 978-0-7614-4889-1
1. Valentine's Day—Juvenile literature. 2. Rebuses—Juvenile literature. I. Title.
GT4925.T78 2010
394.2618—dc22
2009019100

Editor: Christina Gardeski
Publisher: Michelle Bisson
Art Director: Anahid Hamparian
Series Designer: Virginia Pope

Photo research by Connie Gardner
Cover photo by Meg Takamura/*Getty Images*

The photographs in this book are used by permission and through the courtesy of: *Art Life Images*: p. 5 Banana Stock; p. 17 Design Pics; p. 19 Elente Productions. *SuperStock*: p. 9 Geri Lavrov. *Alamy*: p. 11 Norbert Schaefer; p. 15 food folio. *Corbis*: p. 3 RM Mobile, heart; p. 13 Yellow; p. 21 Jose L. Pelaez. *Getty Images*: p. 2 Annie Collinge, balloons; C. Squared Studios, cards; Westend61, chocolates; Lenora Gim, cookies; p. 3 Harrison Eastwood, cupcakes; Eric Bean, lollipops; Dorling Kindersley, sunglasses, p. 7 Jose Luis Pelaez.

Printed in Malaysia (T)
1 3 5 6 4 2